WINNERS
UEFA CHAMPIONS LEAGUE 2022/2023

Man. C... over Inter Milan in the Champions League final — a result which secured a historic treble!

WELCOME!

WOW! IT'S FAIR TO SAY 2023 has been an incredible year of football — full of drama, excitement and incredible achievements. Join us as we take a look back at the biggest moments and celebrate the heroes of the game! Happy reading!

GARY

WHAT'S IN YOUR MOTD MAG ANNUAL?

P10 JUDE BELLINGHAM!

THE BIG WINNERS OF 2023!

MAN. CITY
PREMIER LEAGUE CHAMPIONS

City won their fifth Prem title in six years, despite trailing Arsenal by five points with just two months to go!

MAN. CITY
FA CUP WINNERS

Two weeks after winning the Prem, Pep Guardiola led his team to the double. They beat Man. United 2-1 in the final!

MAN. CITY
CHAMPIONS LEAGUE WINNERS

City made it a historic treble in Istanbul when they beat Inter Milan 1-0 to win the Champions League for the first time!

ERLING HAALAND
PREMIER LEAGUE GOLDEN BOOT

Haaland smashed the Prem's goal record in his first season at the Etihad — he scored 36 goals in just 35 games!

MAN. UNITED
EFL CUP WINNERS

Erik ten Hag got his hands on some silverware in his first season at Old Trafford when his side beat Newcastle 2-0!

96 PAGES OF FOOTY FUN!

WHO'S YOUR G.O.A.T.?

LEGENDS ICONS RIVALS

LIONEL MESSI OR CRISTIANO RONALDO

It's time to decide once and for all who really is the greatest of all time!

P70 MESSI v RONALDO!

THE BEST OF THE BEST!

We reveal the top 30 players in women's football — does YOUR hero make our list?

P86 TOP 30 WOMEN BALLERS!

SUPERSTAR
DREAM TEAM
POSTERS!

Who's made our all-star line-up for 2023? Check out the posters in this annual to find out!

Rule 1: only ONE player per nation!
Rule 2: There is no rule 2!

THE LOL! ZONE!

LIONEL MESSI
ARGENTINA FORWARD

FOOTY STAR REWIND!

We've imagined what today's superstars would have looked like if they'd played 30 years ago!

THOMAS MULLER
GERMANY FORWARD

VIRGIL VAN DIJK
NETHERLANDS CENTRE-BACK

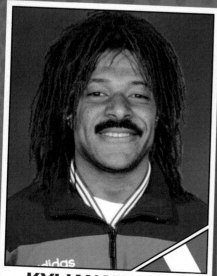

KYLIAN MBAPPE
FRANCE FORWARD

THIBAUT COURTOIS
BELGIUM KEEPER

NEYMAR
BRAZIL FORWARD

ROY'S ANIMAL IMPRESSIONS!

Crystal Palace boss Roy Hodgson is a man of many faces!

HEY ROY... DO YOUR LONG-EARED OWL!

HEY ROY... DO YOUR BABY MACAQUE!

HEY ROY... DO YOUR FRENCH MASTIFF!

HEY ROY... DO YOUR RED PANDA!

HEY ROY... DO YOUR HEDGEHOG!

HEY ROY... DO YOUR MEERKAT!

HEY ROY... DO YOUR SQUIRREL!

THE CHAMPIONS QUIZ!

Ooh, shiny!

These clubs have won the MOST LEAGUE TITLES in their country – but where do they come from?

COLO COLO

1

A Uruguay
B Chile
C Ecuador

GALATASARAY

2

A Bulgaria
B Turkey
C Greece

RIVER PLATE

3

A Mexico
B Brazil
C Argentina

AJAX

4

A Netherlands
B Belgium
C Denmark

ANDERLECHT

5

A Romania
B Belgium
C Switzerland

LINFIELD

6

A Wales
B Northern Ireland
C Republic of Ireland

BENFICA

7

A Spain
B Portugal
C Serbia

JUVENTUS

8

A France
B Germany
C Italy

LA GALAXY

9

A Australia
B USA
C India

YOUR FOOTY BRAIN POWER

YOUR SCORE ☐/9

9	GENIUS
7	PROFESSIONAL
5	SEMI-PRO
3	AMATEUR
1	SUNDAY LEAGUE
0	OH NO, DISASTER

ANSWERS ON PAGE 92!

15 de junio de 2023

HEY JUDE BELLINGHAM

JUDE'S JOURNEY FROM BIRMINGHAM TO THE BERNABEU!

This is the story of a little boy from the Midlands set to become a megastar in Madrid!

THE RECORD BREAKING ROAD TO REAL!

1 THE STORY BEGINS IN STOURBRIDGE IN 2003...

Jude Victor William Bellingham is born on 29 June 2003, in Stourbridge, in the West Midlands. His dad Mark, a police sergeant, was a prolific goalscorer in non-League football — netting more than 700 goals in his playing days!

2 FROM UNDER-8s TO THE CHAMPIONSHIP...

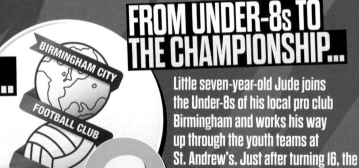

Little seven-year-old Jude joins the Under-8s of his local pro club Birmingham and works his way up through the youth teams at St. Andrew's. Just after turning 16, the talented teenager is handed the No.22 shirt for the 2019-20 Championship season — this is his big chance!

ST. ANDREW'S STAR IS BORN...

3

It doesn't take long for Jude to take that chance. He becomes Birmingham's youngest-ever player when he makes his debut in August 2019, aged only 16. A few weeks later, he also becomes their youngest-ever scorer when he nets a winner against Stoke!

4

Despite playing just 44 games for the club, Birmingham retire the No.22 shirt in Jude's honour!

TIME TO SAY BYE BYE, BLUES...

By the end of the season, he is in demand — Man. United and Borussia Dortmund are battling it out for his signature. Enticed by Dortmund's record of developing young players, he joins them for £25 million in July 2020 — making him the most expensive 17-year-old in history!

DREAM DEBUT...

Jude makes his debut for his new club in the first match of the 2020-21 season — a German Cup match. He stars and scores in a thumping 5-0 win, and it means that, aged just 17, he had become Dortmund's youngest-ever goalscorer!

5

Dortmund, inspired by Bellingham, go on to win the cup that season — it's Jude's first trophy!

6

THE RECORDS CONTINUE TO TUMBLE...

The following month, when Dortmund face Lazio in the Champions League group stage, Bellingham becomes the youngest Englishman to start a UCL match, breaking the record previously set by Phil Foden!

JUDE IS THE REAL DEAL...

7

After three seasons in Germany, in which he wins the German Cup, the Bundesliga Player of the Year, and the hearts of the German fans, he decides to leave Dortmund. In June 2023, he joins Real Madrid for £88.5m — a fee which could eventually rise to £115m. He's made the big time!

JUDE'S PHOTO SCRAPBOOK...

NOVEMBER 2020
He makes his England debut against the Republic of Ireland at Wembley, becoming England's third-youngest player of all time!

JULY 2020
Following his record-breaking move to Borussia Dortmund, a huge mural appears in his home city of Birmingham!

APRIL 2021
Jude celebrates his first Champions League goal in a huge quarter-final clash against Man. City — a strike which sees him become Dortmund and England's youngest UCL scorer!

JUNE 2021
Despite having played just 29 top-flight games, 17-year-old Jude is called up to the England squad for Euro 2020!

JUNE 2021
Jude comes on in England's opening Euro 2020 match, a 1-0 win over Croatia, and becomes the youngest player in the history of the Euros!

DECEMBER 2022
Jude celebrates England's last-16 World Cup win over Senegal in the Al Bayt Stadium. His Three Lions team-mate Phil Foden says: "I think he will be the best midfielder in the world!"

NOVEMBER 2022
Bellers bags his first international goal in England's 6-2 win over Iran at Qatar 2022, making him the second-youngest scorer for England at a World Cup!

MAY 2023
Bellingham laps up the applause after scoring in Borussia Dortmund's 5-2 over Borussia Monchengladbach — it turns out to be his last game for the club!

JUNE 2023
Jude bags his big move to Real Madrid and also bags the No.5 shirt, the number of his childhood idol Zinedine Zidane, who was a legend at the Bernabeu!

HOW TALL

FEET

Take a look to see how you measure up against the world's best ballers — as well as the stars of the animal kingdom!

Get an adult or a mate to measure how tall you are!

MY HEIGHT

FT   INS

11
10
9
8
7
6
5
4
3
2
1
0

KANGAROO
5ft 10in

MOHAMED SALAH
5ft 9in

LIONEL MESSI
5ft 7in

ORANGUTAN
4ft 5in

BISON
5ft 8in

GENTOO
PENGUIN
2ft 6in

16

ARE YOU?

FEET

MARCUS RASHFORD
5ft 11in

SON HEUNG-MIN
6ft 0in

ERLING HAALAND
6ft 4in

OSTRICH
9ft 0in

THIBAUT COURTOIS
6ft 6in

GRIZZLY BEAR
9ft 6in

POLAR BEAR
10ft 0in

11

10

9

8

7

6

5

4

3

2

1

0

DI LORENZO

GIOVANNI

ITALY

THE 5-A-SIDE WORLD CUP!

We've picked the ultimate 5-a-side team from each continent — but how do you rate them?

AFRICA

Andre Onana — CAMEROON
Achraf Hakimi — MOROCCO
Ismael Bennacer — ALGERIA
Mohamed Salah — EGYPT
Victor Osimhen — NIGERIA

Mohamed Salah

ASIA

Mathew Ryan — AUSTRALIA
Kim Min-jae — SOUTH KOREA
Daichi Kamada — JAPAN
Son Heung-Min — SOUTH KOREA
Kaoru Mitoma — JAPAN

Son Heung-Min

EUROPE

Thibaut Courtois — BELGIUM
Ruben Dias — PORTUGAL
Kevin De Bruyne — BELGIUM
Erling Haaland — NORWAY
Kylian Mbappe — FRANCE

Thibaut Courtois

NORTH & CENTRAL AMERICA

Keylor Navas — COSTA RICA
Alphonso Davies — CANADA
Tyler Adams — USA
Christian Pulisic — USA
Jonathan David — CANADA

Tyler Adams

SOUTH AMERICA

Alisson Becker — BRAZIL
Marquinhos — BRAZIL
Casemiro — BRAZIL
Lionel Messi — ARGENTINA
Vinicius Junior — BRAZIL

Casemiro

THE TEAMS RANKED!

Rank the five-a-side teams below in order — starting with the best continent and ending with the worst!

1 ....

2 ....

3 ....

4 ....

5 ....

19

SPOT THE BALL!

We've removed the ball from the *FOUR PREMIER LEAGUE PHOTOS* below – can you guess where it should be?

BALL 1 A B C D E F G
1 2 3 4
ANSWER: ....

BALL 2 A B C D E F G
1 2 3 4
ANSWER: ....

BALL 3 A B C D E F G
1 2 3 4
ANSWER: ....

BALL 4 A B C D E F G
1 2 3 4
ANSWER: ....

STADIUM SEARCH!

Can you find the 12 BRITISH FOOTBALL STADIUMS hiding in the word grid below?

S	T	A	M	F	O	R	D	B	R	I	D	G	E
R	U	H	N	T	I	P	H	V	E	B	W	S	X
L	O	Y	T	G	Q	K	Z	V	T	R	E	D	A
J	D	F	E	E	V	A	P	J	B	O	C	T	E
H	R	X	M	O	L	I	N	E	U	X	R	C	C
Y	O	T	I	R	V	M	C	T	S	P	V	I	E
W	F	R	R	Y	I	T	F	I	D	X	I	T	L
K	F	L	A	M	E	X	E	H	C	Z	L	Y	T
R	A	E	T	D	S	H	K	A	I	U	L	G	I
O	R	U	E	E	D	C	Z	D	M	N	A	R	C
U	T	Y	S	D	F	H	K	L	D	S	P	O	P
M	D	L	D	A	N	F	I	E	L	D	A	U	A
S	L	O	L	G	F	D	U	O	I	Y	R	N	R
G	O	O	D	I	S	O	N	P	A	R	K	D	K

AMEX

ANFIELD

CELTIC PARK

CITY GROUND

EMIRATES

ETIHAD

GOODISON PARK

IBROX

MOLINEUX

OLD TRAFFORD

STAMFORD BRIDGE

VILLA PARK

GUESS WHO!

Name these high-profile FOOTY MANAGERS pictured in their playing days!

1

NAME: ....

2

NAME: ....

3

NAME: ....

4

NAME: ....

ANSWERS ON PAGE 92!

WSL IN

32,262

The biggest stadium in the WSL is the King Power, home of Leicester's women's and men's teams!

2011

The Women's Super League was founded 12 years ago, replacing the old Premier League National as the top tier of women's football in England!

The first winners of the WSL were Arsenal!

12

The number of teams in the WSL — only Arsenal and Chelsea have played in every season!

6

Chelsea's title win last season was their sixth — meaning they've won the league twice as many times as their closest challengers, Arsenal!

WSL TITLE WINS

6	CHELSEA
3	ARSENAL
2	LIVERPOOL
1	MAN. CITY

£300K

Dutch baller Jill Roord became the WSL's most expensive player when she joined Man. City from German side Wolfsburg in July 2023. Midfielder Roord returns to the WSL after playing for Arsenal from 2019 to 2021!

NUMBERS!

42

Arsenal's Beth Mead is the top creator in WSL history — she's clocked up a total of 42 assists for the Gunners and previous club Sunderland!

16 years, 30 days

England star Lauren James became the youngest player in WSL history when she made her debut for Arsenal as a 16-year-old in 2017!

56

Man. United and England keeper Mary Earps has kept a record number of 56 clean sheets in her WSL career — 14 of those came last season as she won the Golden Glove!

Arsenal 11 Bristol City 1

The biggest win in WSL history came in the 2019-20 season — with Netherlands ace Vivianne Miedema scoring six and assisting four of the 11 goals!

78

Superstar striker Vivianne Miedema is the WSL's record goalscorer — she's bagged 78 goals in just 97 games since joining Arsenal in 2017!

MAGIC MIEDEMA!

Most WSL goals in a season: 22 in 2018-19

Most goals in a WSL match: 6 v Bristol City in 2019-20

Most WSL hat-tricks: 5

22

Lioness Rachel Daly netted 22 times for Aston Villa last season — meaning she shares the most goals in a season record with Miedema!

BBC MATCH OF THE DAY MAGAZINE

If you love footy, then you'll love Match of the Day magazine!

+ Packed with the Prem's best ballers and global superstars!

+ Loaded with LOLs, quizzes, activities and epic posters!

+ Bursting with top skills advice, gaming tips and sick boot drops!

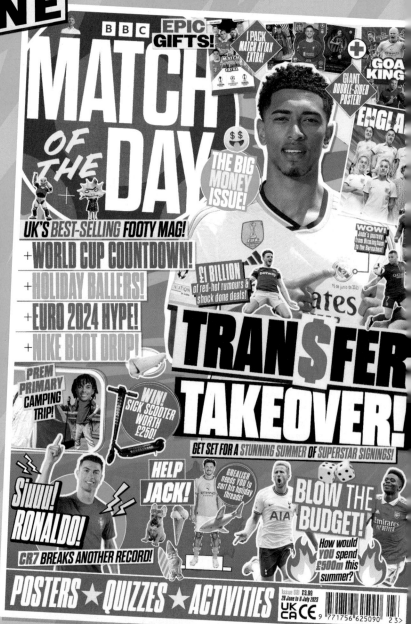

BBC EPIC GIFTS!

MATCH OF THE DAY

1 PACK MATCH ATTAX EXTRA!

GIANT DOUBLE-SIDED POSTER!

GOAL KING

ENGLA

THE BIG MONEY ISSUE!

UK'S BEST-SELLING FOOTY MAG!
+ WORLD CUP COUNTDOWN!
+ HOLIDAY BALLERS!
+ EURO 2024 HYPE!
+ NIKE BOOT DROP!

£1 BILLION of red-hot rumours & shock done deals!

WOW! Jude's journey from Birmingham to the Bernabeu!

TRAN$FER TAKEOVER!

GET SET FOR A STUNNING SUMMER OF SUPERSTAR SIGNINGS!

PREM PRIMARY CAMPING TRIP!

WIN! SICK SCOOTER WORTH £250!

HELP JACK! GREALISH needs you to sort his holiday threads!

Siuuu! RONALDO! CR7 BREAKS ANOTHER RECORD!

BLOW THE BUDGET! How would YOU spend £500m this summer?

POSTERS ★ QUIZZES ★ ACTIVITIES

Issue 081 £3.99
29 June to 8 July 2023

UKCA CE

9 771756 625090   23

FUN-FILLED PAGES FOR YOUNG FOOTY FANS!

ON SALE EVERY FORTNIGHT!

NO.1 MAG FOR WOMEN'S FOOTBALL!

And it tastes delicious!

RUBEN DIAS

PORTUGAL

MATCH OF THE DAY MAGAZINE

WORLD DREAM TEAM!

CENTRE BACK

BADGES & ANIMALS!

Welcome to my zoo!

Can you GUESS THE ENGLISH CLUBS simply by the animals that appear on their badges?

1
A Tottenham
B Bradford
C Stoke

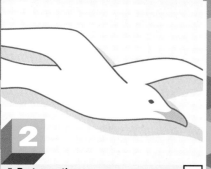

2
A Portsmouth
B Blackpool
C Brighton

3
A Southampton
B Derby
C Ipswich

4
A Coventry
B Reading
C Wycombe

5
A West Brom
B Sheffield Wednesday
C Wigan

6
A Luton
B Leicester
C Hull

7
A Millwall
B Crystal Palace
C Leeds

8
A Watford
B Brentford
C Bristol City

9
A Preston
B Huddersfield
C Burnley

YOUR FOOTY BRAIN POWER

YOUR SCORE ☐ /9

9	GENIUS
7	PROFESSIONAL
5	SEMI-PRO
3	AMATEUR
1	SUNDAY LEAGUE
0	OH NO, DISASTER

ANSWERS ON PAGE 92!

27

GLOBAL FOOTY TOUR....

AFRICA

Countries 54 Area 30,370,000 km2
Total population 1.4 billion
Biggest city Cairo, Egypt
(population 20 million)

FOOTBALL IN AFRICA
FIFA confederation Confederation of African Football (CAF)
CAF HQ Egypt Formed 1957 Member countries 54

THE SUPERSTAR
MOHAMED SALAH
EGYPT

Prolific, record-breaking star who has obliterated Prem and UCL defences over the past six years!

THE LEGEND
SAMUEL ETO'O
CAMEROON

Won three La Liga titles, three UCL trophies and was African Footballer of the Year FOUR times!

MOST SUCCESSFUL NATION
EGYPT
7 x African champions

MOST SUCCESSFUL CLUB
AL AHLY, EGYPT
11 x African champions

ADAM SAYS
Apparently, more than 2,000 different languages are spoken across the continent. Mad!

BIGGEST STADIUM
FNB STADIUM
Johannesburg, South Africa
94,736

ASIA

MOST SUCCESSFUL CLUB
AL-HILAL, SAUDI ARABIA
4 x Asian champions

Countries 49 Area 44,579,000 km2
Total population 4.7 billion
Biggest city Tokyo, Japan
(population 38 million)

FOOTBALL IN ASIA
FIFA confederation Asian Football Confederation (AFC)
AFC HQ Malaysia Formed 1954 Member countries 47

MOST SUCCESSFUL NATION
JAPAN
4 x Asian champions

THE SUPERSTAR
SON HEUNG-MIN
SOUTH KOREA

Dynamic forward who is the top Asian goalscorer in both Premier League and UCL history!

THE LEGEND
ALI DAEI
IRAN

He was the world's top international scorer with 109 goals, until Cristiano Ronaldo broke his record!

ADAM SAYS
Asia's most deadly creature is not the tiger, snake or crocodile — it's the mosquito!

BIGGEST STADIUM
RUNGRADO MAY DAY STADIUM
Pyongyang, North Korea
114,000

EUROPE

Countries 50 Area 10,180,000 km2 Total population 742 million
Biggest city Istanbul, Turkey (population 15.8 million)

FOOTBALL IN EUROPE
FIFA confederation Union of European Football Associations (UEFA)
UEFA HQ Switzerland Formed 1954 Member countries 55

THE SUPERSTAR
KYLIAN MBAPPE
FRANCE

The French star looks set to dominate football for the next decade with his pace and fire finishing!

THE LEGEND
CRISTIANO RONALDO
PORTUGAL

Has scored more than 800 career goals, won five Ballons d'Or, five UCL titles and is international football's record goalscorer!

BIGGEST STADIUM
NOU CAMP
Barcelona, Spain
99,354

MOST SUCCESSFUL NATION
GERMANY
4 x World Cup winners
3 x Euros winners

ADAM SAYS
Almost 90 million tourists visit France each year, making it the world's most visited country! Zut alors!

MOST SUCCESSFUL CLUB
REAL MADRID, SPAIN
14 x European champions

NORTH AMERICA

Countries 23 Area 24,709,000 km2
Total population 604 million
Biggest city Mexico City, Mexico
(population 21.8 million)

BIGGEST STADIUM
AZTEC STADIUM
Mexico City, Mexico
87,523

THE SUPERSTAR
ALPHONSO DAVIES
CANADA

One of the quickest players around today, the left-back is vital for club and country in both defence and attack!

THE LEGEND
HUGO SANCHEZ
MEXICO

Famed for his acrobatic overhead kicks, he bagged 208 goals in 283 games for Spanish giants Real Madrid!

MOST SUCCESSFUL CLUB
CLUB AMERICA, MEXICO
7 x CONCACAF champions

MOST SUCCESSFUL NATION
MEXICO
11 x CONCACAF champions

ADAM SAYS
Americans love a burger — they munch through 50 BILLION every year. Wow!

FOOTBALL IN NORTH AMERICA
FIFA confederation Confederation of North, Central American And Caribbean Association Football (CONCACAF) CONCACAF HQ USA Formed 1961 Member countries 41

OCEANIA

FOOTBALL IN OCEANIA
FIFA confederation Oceania Football Confederation (OFC) OFC HQ New Zealand Formed 1966 Member countries 13

Countries 14 Area 8,526,000 km2
Total population 44 million
Biggest city Sydney, Australia
(population 5 million)

THE SUPERSTAR
MATHEW RYAN
AUSTRALIA

Having played at three World Cups, in La Liga and the Prem, the keeper is the current Australia captain!

THE LEGEND
TIM CAHILL
AUSTRALIA

The attacking midfielder is Australia's record goalscorer, after netting 50 goals in 108 games!

MOST SUCCESSFUL CLUB
AUCKLAND CITY, NEW ZEALAND
7 x OFC champions

MOST SUCCESSFUL NATION
NEW ZEALAND
5 x Oceania champions

ADAM SAYS
Australia quit the OFC in 2006 to join the Asian Confederation, for a better chance of qualifying for World Cups!

BIGGEST STADIUM
STADIUM AUSTRALIA
Sydney, Australia
83,500

SOUTH AMERICA

Countries 12 Area 17,840,000 km2
Total population 441 million
Biggest city Sao Paulo, Brazil
(population 22 million)

BIGGEST STADIUM
ESTADIO MONUMENTAL
Buenos Aires, Argentina
83,198

THE SUPERSTAR

LIONEL MESSI
ARGENTINA

Quite simply the Greatest Of All Time, the 36-year-old has won a record SEVEN Ballon d'Or awards, almost 40 club trophies and scored more than 800 career goals!

THE LEGEND

PELE BRAZIL

Legends don't get much bigger than footy's first superstar. The Brazilian baller scored more than 1,200 goals and won three World Cups — a record!

MOST SUCCESSFUL NATION
BRAZIL
5 x World Cup winners
9 x Copa America winners

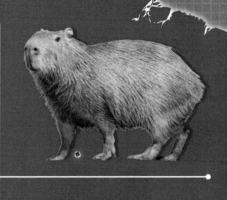

MOST SUCCESSFUL CLUB
INDEPENDIENTE, ARGENTINA
7 x South American champions

ADAM SAYS
On Google it says in parts of South America, they eat llama... what? Eek! Taxi for me, I think!

33

NETHERLANDS

WORLD DREAM TEAM!
CENTRE BACK

VAN DIJK

WOULD YOU RATHER...?

Grab a mate and tackle these *SIX HUGE* footballing dilemmas!

WIN THE WORLD CUP! OR **WIN £5 MILLION ON THE LOTTERY!**

BE A SQUAD PLAYER AT MAN. CITY! OR **BE A STAR PLAYER FOR BOURNEMOUTH!**

MISS A PENALTY IN A SHOOTOUT! OR **SCORE AN OWN GOAL IN A FINAL!**

HAVE A SAUSAGE ROLL FOR A NOSE! OR **HAVE HALF-TIME FRIES FOR HAIR!**

BE A PREMIER LEAGUE HERO! OR **BE A MARVEL SUPERHERO!**

BE A CAT BUT AMAZING AT FOOTBALL! OR **BE A HUMAN BUT RUBBISH AT FOOTBALL!**

35

YOUR AMAZING FOOTY CAREER!

Fill in the blank boxes to map out your epic footy journey from wonderkid to legend!

STEP 1

YOU'RE 14 YEARS OLD...
After starring for your school and junior team, your local Football League club scouts you and invites you to join their academy!

[WRITE YOUR CLOSEST EFL CLUB NAME HERE]

....

STEP 2

YOU MAKE YOUR EFL DEBUT AT 17...
And after three seasons of dazzling displays and media hype, your club accepts an £8m bid and you move to your nearest Premier League club!

[WRITE YOUR NEAREST PREM CLUB NAME HERE]

....

STEP 3

AFTER TWO SENSATIONAL SEASONS...
You've put in sick performances every week, and you're linked with a big money move to a Prem giant. Every club wants you — choose any one you want!

[WRITE YOUR CHOSEN PREM CLUB NAME HERE]

....

STEP 4

YOU'RE A STAR FOR CLUB & COUNTRY...
You're 28 and ready for a new challenge abroad. You are wanted by every UCL superclub in Europe — take your pick of which team to join in a mega £120m deal!

[WRITE YOUR CHOSEN UCL CLUB NAME HERE]

....

STEP 5

YOU'RE A FOOTY ICON...
After four seasons of UCL and league success, and winning the Ballon d'Or twice, you're 32 years old and thinking about quitting elite level footy. You make a £20m move to a Europa League team!

[WRITE YOUR CHOSEN UEL CLUB NAME HERE]

....

STEP 6

AFTER AN INJURY-HIT TWO SEASONS...
You're now 34 years old and starting to wind down your career. You decide to leave European footy and join an MLS team in the USA for a season!

[WRITE YOUR CHOSEN MLS CLUB NAME HERE]

....

STEP 7

AFTER A CAREER OF SUCCESS...
You've won 100 caps, the UCL, several leagues titles and the Ballon d'Or — you decide to return for two final seasons with an EFL club before retiring!

[WRITE YOUR CHOSEN EFL CLUB NAME HERE]

....

Alphonso **Davies**

WORLD DREAM TEAM!
LEFT-BACK

Canada

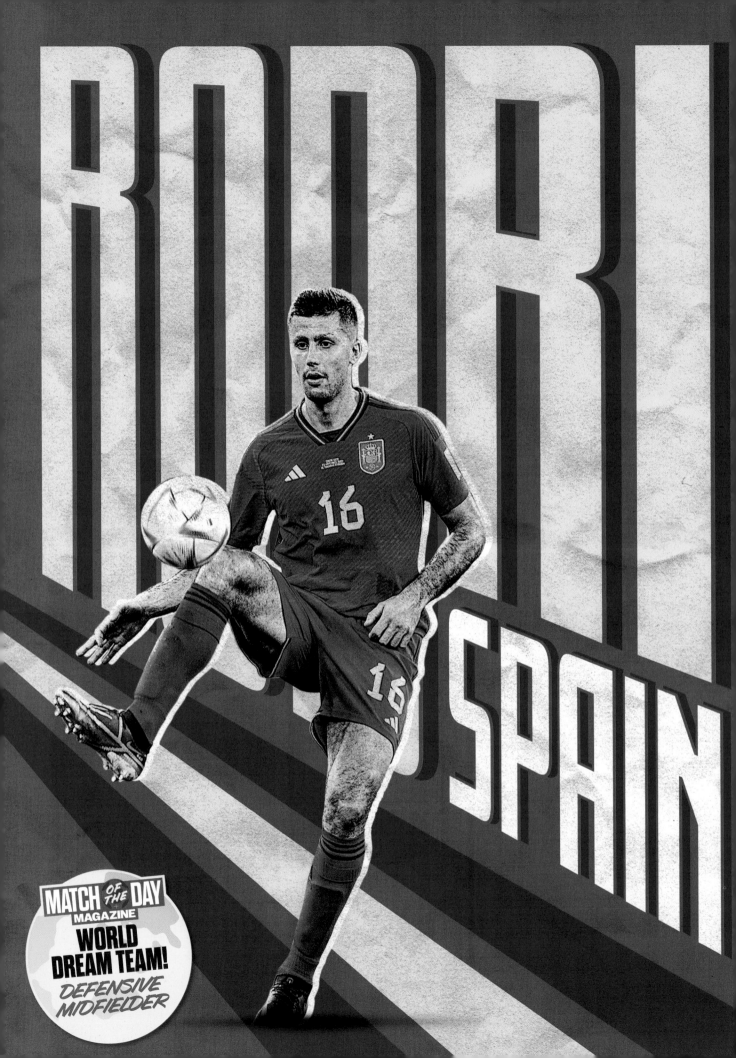

RODRI

SPAIN

MATCH OF THE DAY MAGAZINE

WORLD DREAM TEAM!

DEFENSIVE MIDFIELDER

A YEAR IN FOOTBALL!

How much can you remember about FOOTY IN 2023? It's time to find out!

1 Who won last season's EFL Cup back in February?

A Newcastle
B Man. City
C Man. United

2 What was the score in the 2022-23 FA Cup final?

A Man. City 1-0 Man. United
B Man. City 2-1 Man. United
C Man. City 3-1 Man. United

3 Who finished bottom of the Premier League last season?

A Southampton
B Leicester
C Leeds

4 Who was sacked as Everton boss back in January 2023?

A Patrick Vieira
B Frank Lampard
C Nathan Jones

5 Who did West Ham beat in the Europa Conference League final?

A Sampdoria
B Fiorentina
C AZ Alkmaar

6 Which club won La Liga last season?

A Real Madrid
B Barcelona
C Sevilla

7 Who scored the only goal of the game in the UCL final?

A Erling Haaland
B Rodri
C Ilkay Gundogan

8 Who was top scorer in the WSL last season?

A Sam Kerr
B Rachel Daly
C Alessia Russo

9 Who became Arsenal's record signing in July 2023?

A Jurrien Timber
B Kai Havertz
C Declan Rice

YOUR FOOTY BRAIN POWER

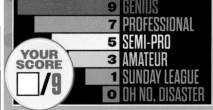

YOUR SCORE ☐/9

9	GENIUS
7	PROFESSIONAL
5	SEMI-PRO
3	AMATEUR
1	SUNDAY LEAGUE
0	OH NO, DISASTER

ANSWERS ON PAGE 92!

+ TOP TEN

GOALS TO SCORE!

From heroic headers to brilliant bicycle kicks, we count down the best types of goal before revealing our No.1!

+ THE ONE-ON-ONE!

10

■ You've timed your run to perfection and you're in on goal with only the keeper to beat. They're racing off their line to narrow the angle — time for deep breaths, a cool head and then either a) slot it low into the corner, b) dink it over them, or c) go round them!

THE MASTER: KYLIAN MBAPPE

DIFFICULTY RATING: 5/10

WOW FACTOR: 🔥🔥

SCORED IT! ✓

+ THE BULLET HEADER!

9

■ There are loads of different types of headers: glancing, cushioned, looping, diving — but our favourite is the thumping bullet header that rockets into the back of the net. It's all about a giant leap, a perfect connection and bulging neck muscles to get the power!

THE MASTER: HARRY KANE

DIFFICULTY RATING: 6/10

WOW FACTOR: 🔥🔥🔥

SCORED IT! ✓

+ THE TEAM GOAL!

8

This may end up being a simple tap-in from two yards out, but it's what has gone before that makes this special. Pep Guardiola teams are the kings of the pass-and-move and often make 30 passes or more before hitting the net. It takes all 11 players to be on the same page!

THE MASTER: MAN. CITY

DIFFICULTY RATING: 6/10

WOW FACTOR: 🔥🔥🔥🔥🔥

SCORED IT! ✓

+ THE CHEEKY CHIP!

7

This one is proof that a wondergoal doesn't have to be all about power. This delicate dink often flies through the air in slow motion, but all the back-peddling or wrong-footed keeper can do is watch it sail over them before it nestles in the back of the net!

THE MASTER: MOHAMED SALAH

DIFFICULTY RATING: 7/10

WOW FACTOR: 🔥🔥🔥🔥🔥

SCORED IT! ✓

✛ THE PANENKA!

6

■ How can a penalty be one of the best goals you can score? Well, it's the King of Penalties. Named after Antonin Panenka, who did this pen for the first time at Euro '76, this is about faking you're going to blast it into the corner, but instead delicately dink it down the middle!

THE MASTER: KARIM BENZEMA

DIFFICULTY RATING: 8/10

WOW FACTOR: 🔥🔥🔥🔥🔥

SCORED IT!

✛ THE TOP BINS BOMB!

5

■ Goals from outside the box come in all shapes and sizes, and nothing looks more spectacular than hitting top bins from 30 yards out. This requires great technique, accuracy and a super-charged boot to make sure it fizzes into the top corner past the despairing keeper!

THE MASTER: KEVIN DE BRUYNE

DIFFICULTY RATING: 8/10

WOW FACTOR: 🔥🔥🔥🔥🔥

SCORED IT!

+ THE SICK FREE-KICK!

4

■ Bending a 25-yard free-kick into the top corner is one of football's greatest sights, but it's pretty rare to see. Getting the ball up and over a five-man wall is harder than it looks. You need concentration and technique to find the perfect balance of accuracy and power!

THE MASTER: MARCUS RASHFORD

DIFFICULTY RATING: 8/10

WOW FACTOR: 🔥🔥🔥🔥🔥

SCORED IT! ✔

+ THE HUGE VOLLEY!

3

■ Another glorious sight, and one which leaves fans in awe. This requires unbelievable tekkers and co-ordination to ensure there's a clean connection and that the ball doesn't go flying over the bar. Always a goal of the season contender if executed to perfection!

THE MASTER: ROBERT LEWANDOWSKI

DIFFICULTY RATING: 8/10

WOW FACTOR: 🔥🔥🔥🔥🔥

SCORED IT! ✔

+ THE SOLO DRIBBLE!

2

A feint, a stepover, a side-step, a burst of acceleration, a shimmy, another stepover, another feint, a nutmeg and then a cool-as-you-like side-foot into the far corner... wow. The mazy dribble followed by a clinical finish is so tough, and that's what makes it so special!

THE MASTER: LIONEL MESSI

DIFFICULTY RATING: 9/10

WOW FACTOR: 🔥🔥🔥🔥🔥

SCORED IT!

+ THE OVERHEAD KICK!

1

This is the goal that everyone dreams of scoring! The acrobatic overhead kick should be framed and put in an art gallery — it's a thing of beauty. As the player leaps into the air, time stops before... BOOM the connection and then the ball rockets past the helpless keeper!

THE MASTER: ERLING HAALAND

DIFFICULTY RATING: 10/10

WOW FACTOR: 🔥🔥🔥🔥🔥

SCORED IT!

JUDE

BELLINGHAM

ENGLAND

QUIZ

BIG MONEY MEN!

Jackpot!

Which player holds the record for being his country's MOST EXPENSIVE ever transfer?

ARGENTINA

1
- **A** Lionel Messi
- **B** Enzo Fernandez
- **C** Lautaro Martinez

PORTUGAL

2
- **A** Luis Figo
- **B** Cristiano Ronaldo
- **C** Joao Felix

ITALY

3
- **A** Roberto Baggio
- **B** Sandro Tonali
- **C** Jorginho

NETHERLANDS

4
- **A** Frenkie de Jong
- **B** Virgil van Dijk
- **C** Arjen Robben

GERMANY

5
- **A** Kai Havertz
- **B** Ilkay Gundogan
- **C** Joshua Kimmich

SCOTLAND

6
- **A** John McGinn
- **B** Andy Robertson
- **C** Kieran Tierney

NORWAY

7
- **A** Erling Haaland
- **B** Martin Odegaard
- **C** Sander Berge

SPAIN

8
- **A** Andres Iniesta
- **B** Kepa Arrizabalaga
- **C** Rodri

SOUTH KOREA

9
- **A** Son Heung-min
- **B** Kim Min-jae
- **C** Park Ji-sung

YOUR FOOTY BRAIN POWER

YOUR SCORE ☐ /9

- **9** GENIUS
- **7** PROFESSIONAL
- **5** SEMI-PRO
- **3** AMATEUR
- **1** SUNDAY LEAGUE
- **0** OH NO, DISASTER

ANSWERS ON PAGE 92!

BARCELONA
LA LIGA CHAMPIONS

2022-23

NAPOLI
SERIE A CHAMPIONS

CHELSEA
WSL CHAMPIONS

PSG
LIGUE 1 CHAMPIONS

CELTIC
SCOTTISH PREMIERSHIP
CHAMPIONS

BAYERN MUNICH
BUNDESLIGA CHAMPIONS

AGUE
NERS

YOU ARE A...

SUPERSTAR

BALLER!

How would YOU spend £500m on your dream superstar life — it's time to make some BIG decisions!

NAME:
....

AGE: NICKNAME:
....

HEIGHT: WEIGHT:
....

POSITION:
....

SIGNATURE:
....

Stick your photo here and fill in your baller fact file!

Give yourself a sick autograph!

WHAT YOU NEED TO DO!

1 Work through the 11 sections over the next seven pages.

2 Choose ONE option for each category.

3 You can't go over your £500m budget, so keep a note of how much you're spending.

4 When you've made your choices, cut them out and stick them into the correct place on p60-61.

ASK AN ADULT TO HELP YOU WITH THE CUTTING!

① THE STADIUM
Which ground do you want to play in?

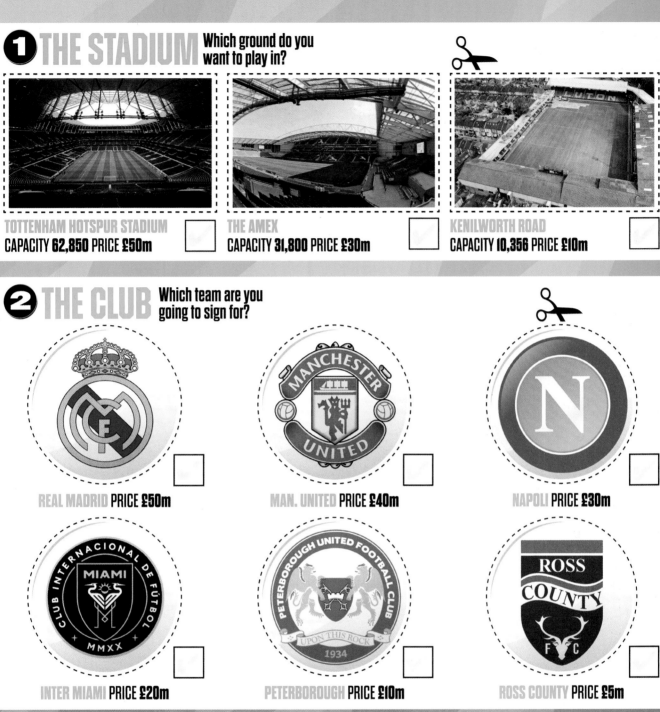

TOTTENHAM HOTSPUR STADIUM
CAPACITY **62,850** PRICE **£50m**

THE AMEX
CAPACITY **31,800** PRICE **£30m**

KENILWORTH ROAD
CAPACITY **10,356** PRICE **£10m**

② THE CLUB
Which team are you going to sign for?

REAL MADRID PRICE **£50m**

MAN. UNITED PRICE **£40m**

NAPOLI PRICE **£30m**

INTER MIAMI PRICE **£20m**

PETERBOROUGH PRICE **£10m**

ROSS COUNTY PRICE **£5m**

③ THE MANAGER
Which boss do you want to play under?

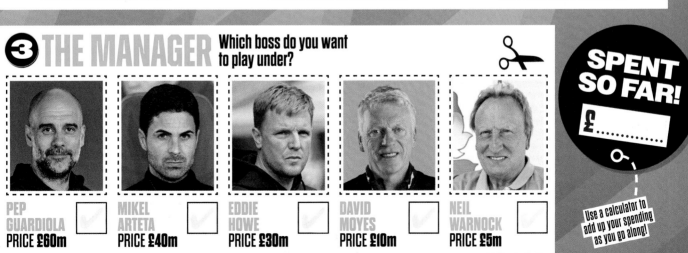

PEP GUARDIOLA PRICE **£60m**

MIKEL ARTETA PRICE **£40m**

EDDIE HOWE PRICE **£30m**

DAVID MOYES PRICE **£10m**

NEIL WARNOCK PRICE **£5m**

SPENT SO FAR!
£............

Use a calculator to add up your spending as you go along!

★

BALLER LIFE

MOHAMED SALAH

Mo, who is sponsored by brands like Adidas, Pepsi and Uber, has made huge donations to improve the lives of people in Egypt!

★

BALLER LIFE

ROBERT LEWANDOWSKI

Nike athlete and FIFA cover star Lewy has donated and raised money for loads of charitable organisations throughout his career!

④ YOUR SQUAD
Time to assemble your awesome crew!

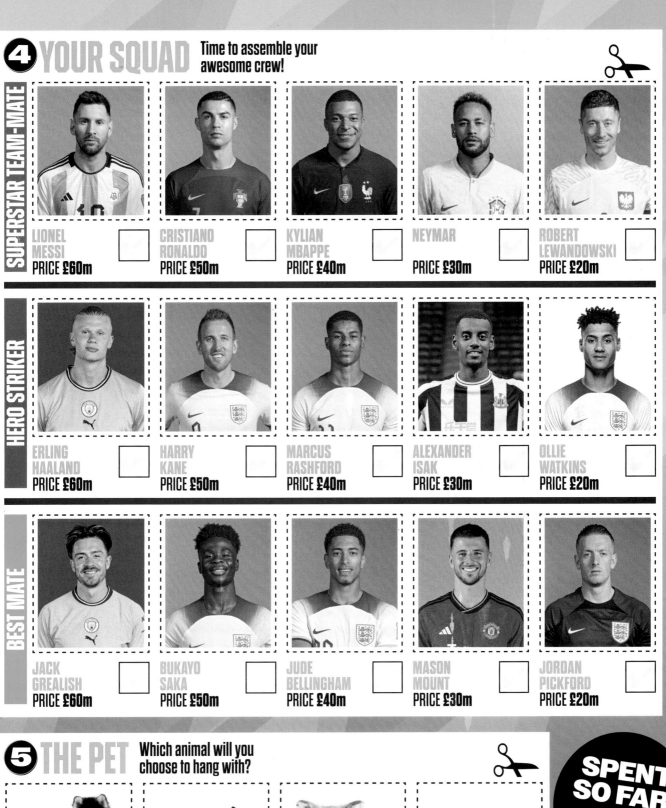

SUPERSTAR TEAM-MATE

LIONEL MESSI	CRISTIANO RONALDO	KYLIAN MBAPPE	NEYMAR	ROBERT LEWANDOWSKI
PRICE £60m	PRICE £50m	PRICE £40m	PRICE £30m	PRICE £20m

HERO STRIKER

ERLING HAALAND	HARRY KANE	MARCUS RASHFORD	ALEXANDER ISAK	OLLIE WATKINS
PRICE £60m	PRICE £50m	PRICE £40m	PRICE £30m	PRICE £20m

BEST MATE

JACK GREALISH	BUKAYO SAKA	JUDE BELLINGHAM	MASON MOUNT	JORDAN PICKFORD
PRICE £60m	PRICE £50m	PRICE £40m	PRICE £30m	PRICE £20m

⑤ THE PET
Which animal will you choose to hang with?

DOG	CAT	HAMSTER	GOLDFISH
PRICE £30m	PRICE £20m	PRICE £10m	PRICE £5m

SPENT SO FAR!

£ ....

Use a calculator to add up your spending as you go along!

BALLER LIFE
MARCUS RASHFORD

Rashy's high-profile campaigning and donations have helped combat homelessness, child food poverty and improve literacy!

BALLER LIFE
KYLIAN MBAPPE

Kyl brings in millions from deals with Nike, Hublot and Oakley, but he's also donated millions to good causes during that time!

6 THE SHIRT NUMBER
Pick your squad number for the season!

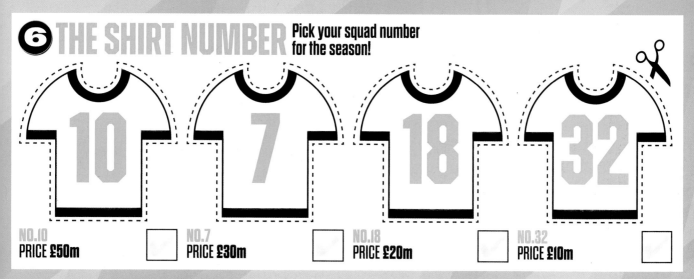

NO.10
PRICE £50m

NO.7
PRICE £30m

NO.18
PRICE £20m

NO.32
PRICE £10m

7 THE CAR
Choose the whip you'll ride around in!

BUGATTI
PRICE £50m

PORSCHE
PRICE £30m

HONDA
PRICE £20m

MINI
PRICE £10m

8 THE HOUSE
Select where you're going to chill after games!

MANSION
PRICE £50m

MODERN
PRICE £40m

BUNGALOW
PRICE £20m

CARAVAN
PRICE £10m

SPENT SO FAR!
£ ....

Use a calculator to add up your spending as you go along!

★
BALLER LIFE
HARRY KANE

Harry launched the Harry Kane Foundation in 2022 to help change people's out-dated thinking about mental health!

★
BALLER LIFE
BUKAYO SAKA

Saka earns loads from his boot deal, but he's also happy giving to charity. Last year he funded 120 life-changing operations!

⑨ THE SPONSORSHIP
Which big-money deal are you going to accept?

EA FC COVER STAR
PRICE £50m ☐

ODEON INFLUENCER
PRICE £30m ☐

FACE OF CLARKS SHOES
PRICE £20m ☐

GREGGS AMBASSADOR
PRICE £10m ☐

⑩ THE BOOT DEAL
Pick the wheels that you'll ball in!

NIKE
PRICE £50m ☐

PUMA
PRICE £30m ☐

UMBRO
PRICE £20m ☐

CONCAVE
PRICE £10m ☐

⑪ THE CHARITY DONATION
How much money will you give to good causes? ✂

HUGE DONATION
PRICE £50m ☐

DECENT DONATION
PRICE £40m ☐

SMALL DONATION
PRICE £20m ☐

TINY DONATION
PRICE £10m ☐

SPENT SO FAR!

£ ....

Use a calculator to add up your spending as you go along!

★ **BALLER LIFE**

LIONEL MESSI

Leo has sponsorship deals with Adidas, Pepsi and Mastercard. He's a UNICEF ambassador and has his own charitable foundation!

★ **BALLER LIFE**

CRISTIANO RONALDO

CR7 is a multi-million pound brand, he's Nike's A-list athlete and he's donated millions to charity during his 20-year career!

MY BALLER LIFE

You've made your choices, now it's time to glue your selections in place and put your new pro baller lifestyle together!

YOUR STADIUM

YOUR CLUB

Stick your baller fact file here!

YOUR SQUAD

YOUR MANAGER

Slurp!

SUPERSTAR TEAM-MATE

HERO STRIKER

BEST MATE

YOUR PET

YOUR SHIRT NUMBER

YOUR CAR

YOUR HOUSE

YOUR SPONSOR

YOUR BOOTS

YOUR CHARITY DONATION

FINAL SPEND!

£.................

20
THINGS YOU NEED TO KNOW ABOUT
EURO 2024!

The ultimate guide to next summer's huge tournament!

1

IT'S BEING HELD IN GERMANY!

Yep, Germany will host Euro 2024, the 17th European Championship. The Euros were held in West Germany in 1988, but this will be the first time the country has staged the Euros since reunification!

HISTORY LESSON!

Between 1949 and 1990, Germany was divided into two countries — West Germany and East Germany.

2 WHEN IS EURO 2024? 14

The tournament will last a whole month and takes place from 14 June to 14 July 2024. Berlin will host the final on Sunday 14 July 2024, while the tourney kicks off in Munich on Friday 14 June!

THERE ARE 10 HOST CITIES! 3

Ten amazing stadiums will be hosting games at Euro 2024. These venues are:

BERLIN
Olympiastadion
70,000

COLOGNE
Cologne Stadium
47,000

DORTMUND
BVB Stadion
66,000

DUSSELDORF
Dusseldorf Arena
47,000

FRANKFURT
Frankfurt Arena
46,000

GELSENKIRCHEN
Arena AufSchalke
50,000

HAMBURG
Volksparkstadion
50,000

LEIPZIG
Leipzig Stadium
42,000

MUNICH
Munich Football Arena
67,000

STUTTGART
Stuttgart Arena
54,000

4 SO HOW MANY TEAMS WILL BE THERE?

In total, 24 teams will take part. Germany qualify as hosts, 20 nations will earn their place at the finals via the qualification group stage and three more will join through the playoffs!

HOW WILL IT WORK? 5

There will be six groups, with the top two in each group qualifying for the knockout stage, along with the four best third-placed finishers!

9

UNITED BY FOOTBALL!

The tournament's official slogan is: 'United by Football. Vereint im Herzen Europas'. For those who don't speak German, the second part of the slogan is: 'United in the heart of Europe!'

6

BRING ON BERLIN!

The Euro 2024 final will be held at Berlin's Olympiastadion, Germany's biggest stadium. It hosted the 2006 World Cup final, the 2015 Champions League final and is the home of Hertha Berlin, who were relegated from the Bundesliga last season!

10

FRANCE SHOULD WIN IT!

France have already been named as the team to beat. After their epic penalty shootout defeat to Argentina in last year's World Cup final in Qatar, Kylian Mbappe and his mates will want to prove they're Europe's No.1!

MEET THE MASCOT!

The official mascot for Euro 2024 is a bear called Albärt! Over the years, tournament mascots have included a rabbit called Berni, a lion named Goliath and a cockerel called Peno — but this is the first bear!

8

7

ITALY ARE THE REIGNING CHAMPS!

Who can forget the Euro 2020 final? England versus Italy, Wembley Stadium, the hosts dreaming of their first trophy since 1966 — but it was the Italians who won it thanks to a dramatic 3-2 penalty shootout!

11

EURO KINGS!

Germany and Spain are the two most successful nations in Euros history, both winning the title three times. In fact, ten countries have won the European Championship since it was introduced in 1960!

TEAM	WINS
GERMANY	3 (1972, 1980, 1996)
SPAIN	3 (1964, 2008, 2012)
ITALY	2 (1968, 2020)
FRANCE	2 (1984, 2000)
RUSSIA	1 (1960)
CZECH REPUBLIC	1 (1976)
PORTUGAL	1 (2016)
NETHERLANDS	1 (1988)
DENMARK	1 (1992)
GREECE	1 (2004)

12

MUNICH OPENER!

The Munich Football Arena, home to Bayern Munich, will host the opening ceremony and the first match of Euro 2024. Almost 70,000 fans will be packed into the iconic stadium for the tournament's kick-off, which will feature host nation Germany!

TALE OF THE TROPHY!

13 The Henri Delaunay trophy, which is awarded to the winner of the European Championships, is named after, well, Henri Delaunay. Henners was the first General Secretary of UEFA and the bloke who came up with the idea for the tournament!

The trophy weighs 8kg and is 60cm tall — the same height and weight as a Rhesus monkey!

GOLDEN BOOT!

As ever, the race for the Golden Boot promises to be sensational. Some of Europe's hottest strikers will go head-to-head in Germany next summer, but can any of them better French legend Michel Platini's tournament record? His nine goals at Euro 84 fired France to glory on home soil!

14

Fernando Torres was a joint winner in 2012

15

SCOTLAND EXPECTS!

Scotland failed to win a single game at the last Euros, although they did hold England to a 0-0 draw at Wembley. The Tartan Army have NEVER made it out of the group stage at a European Championship — can Steve Clarke's lads finally end that dismal record in Germany next summer?

16

THE EUROS GOAT!

Portugal superstar Cristiano Ronaldo holds a ridiculous number of European Championship records. He made his Euros debut in 2004 — and he hasn't looked back!

RONALDO'S RECORDS!		
Most tournaments	5	(2004, 2008, 2012, 2016, 2020)
Most matches played	25	
Most matches won	12	
Most goals scored	14	

17

WORLD CUP MEMS!

The last time a football tournament was held in Germany was the 2006 World Cup, 18 years ago — and it was pure drama. England crashed out on penalties to Portugal in the quarter-finals, and France suffered penalty heartbreak in the final as Zinedine Zidane was sent off before they lost their shootout to Italy!

18

HOME SWEET HOME!

On the 12 occasions a Euros has been staged in a single country, the hosts have always made at least the semis, and have gone on to win it three times — Spain (1964), Italy (1968) and France (1984). Will Germany add their name to that list next summer?

19

GERMAN BANGERS!

If you love a sausage, this is the Euros for you. Germany is home to around 1,200 different types of banger, including the Bratwurst, Frankfurter, Weisswurst and Wollwurst!

20

ENGLAND'S DREAM OR NIGHTMARE!

Gareth Southgate's team were a penalty kick away from winning Euro 2020, but it wasn't to be. This will be their 11th Euros and they go into it as one of the favourites. One note of caution, though — the last time the Three Lions played in the Euros on German soil, at Euro 88, they lost every game!

TOP BOTTOM TRUMPS!

BONKERS BADGES EDITION!

AVENIR BEGGEN
LUXEMBOURG

Club founded	1915
Bearded pixies	1
Footballs	1
Weirdness	79%
Rubbishness	65%
Cool factor	65%
BONKERS RATING	**88%**

DID YOU KNOW?
Avenir Beggen's nickname is Wichtelcher, which translates as the Pixies. These creatures are small and mischievous and known for playing tricks on people!

Is that a goblin?

AVENIR SPORTIF DE LA MARSA
TUNISIA

المستقبل الرياضي بالمرسى
AVENIR SPORTIF DE LA MARSA
1939

Club founded	1939
Bendy camels	1
Footballs	1
Weirdness	76%
Rubbishness	66%
Cool factor	43%
BONKERS RATING	**76%**

DID YOU KNOW?
Arabian camels can smell water from about 50 miles away — which can come in pretty handy if you're trudging through the desert with a massive thirst on!

CHANGCHUN YATAI FC
CHINA

YATAI FOOTBALL
长春亚泰
1996

Club founded	1996
Ducks with antlers	1
Footballs	1
Weirdness	88%
Rubbishness	46%
Cool factor	48%
BONKERS RATING	**89%**

DID YOU KNOW?
Changchun Yatai won the Chinese Super League by just a single point back in 2007, but the club from north-east China have failed to hit those heights since!

ARAGUAINA

BRAZIL

Club founded	1997
Confused cows	1
Canoes	1
Weirdness	89%
Rubbishness	88%
Cool factor	28%
BONKERS RATING	86%

DID YOU KNOW?

Araguaina is in rural Brazil, and is famous for cattle farming. The club's nickname 'Tourão do Norte' translates as 'The Big Bull of the North'. And they love a canoe!

ASFA YENNENGA

BURKINA FASO

Club founded	1947
White horses	1
Bow and arrows	1
Weirdness	79%
Rubbishness	56%
Cool factor	33%
BONKERS RATING	62%

DID YOU KNOW?

According to Burkina Faso folklore, Yennenga was a legendary warrior princess, who lived over 900 years ago. Loads of statues of her can be found in the country's capital!

AS PONTA LESTE

EAST TIMOR

Club founded	1991
Friendly crocodiles	1
Footballs	1
Weirdness	65%
Rubbishness	69%
Cool factor	22%
BONKERS RATING	70%

DID YOU KNOW?

East Timor, also known as Timor-Leste, is an island 400 miles north of Australia — and according to local legend, the island was formed out of a giant crocodile!

COBRESAL

CHILE

Club founded	1979
Miner's hats	1
Footballs	1
Weirdness	72%
Rubbishness	76%
Cool factor	38%
BONKERS RATING	71%

DID YOU KNOW?

The club is based in El Salvador, a mining town in Chile. It's in the middle of the Atacama Desert, parts of which have NEVER had any rain!

CHICKEN INN FC

ZIMBABWE

Club founded	1997
Chickens	1
Footballs	1
Weirdness	55%
Rubbishness	70%
Cool factor	40%
BONKERS RATING	59%

DID YOU KNOW?

The club comes from Bulawayo, Zimbabwe's second largest city — but gets its unusual name from a fast-food restaurant, whose slogan is: Luv dat chicken!

WHO'S YOUR

LIONEL

MESSI

OR

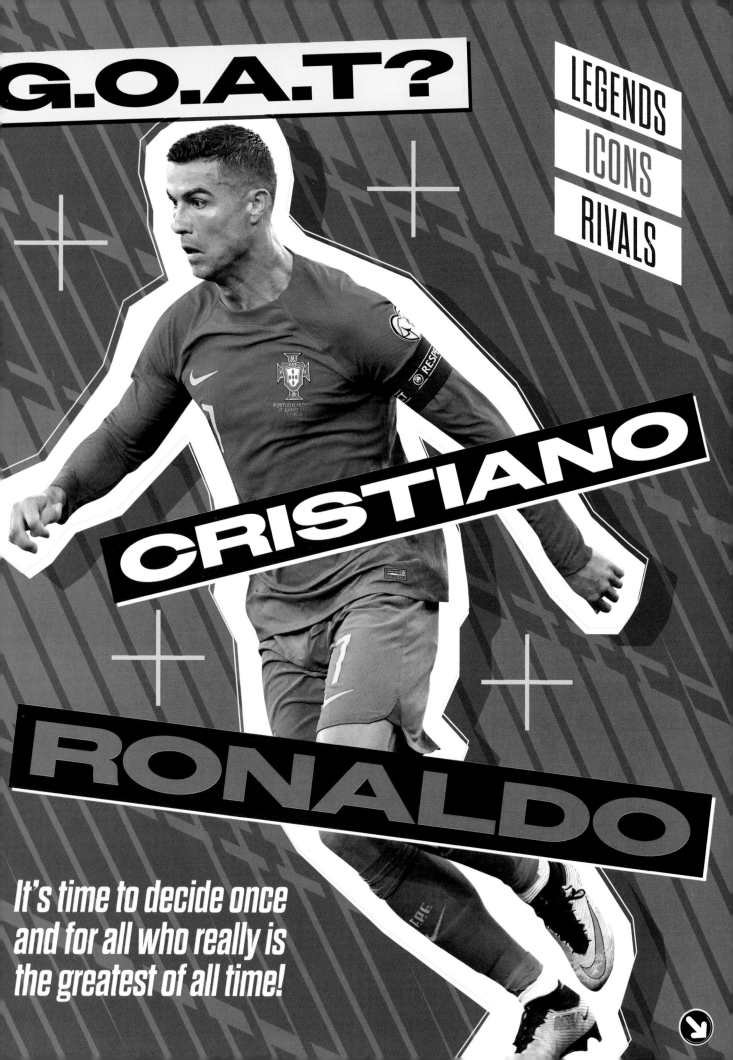

G.O.A.T?

**LEGENDS
ICONS
RIVALS**

CRISTIANO
RONALDO

It's time to decide once and for all who really is the greatest of all time!

He exploded onto the scene 20 years ago. He's won more Ballons d'Or than anyone. He's a legend at Barcelona and led his nation to World Cup glory last year. He is...

LIONEL MESSI

BORN 1987 AGE 36

BIRTHPLACE ROSARIO ARGENTINA

MAJOR TROPHIES

- **1** World Cup
- **1** Copa America
- **4** Champions League
- **10** La Liga
- **2** Ligue 1
- **7** Copa del Rey
- **3** FIFA Club World Cup
- **3** UEFA Super Cup

TOTAL TROPHIES
40

PRO DEBUT: 2004

CLUB	COUNTRY
855 GAMES	**175** GAMES
707 GOALS	**103** GOALS

TOTAL
1,030 GAMES 810 GOALS
1 GOAL EVERY 1.27 GAMES

2004-21 672 GOALS

2021-23 32 GOALS

2023- 3 GOALS

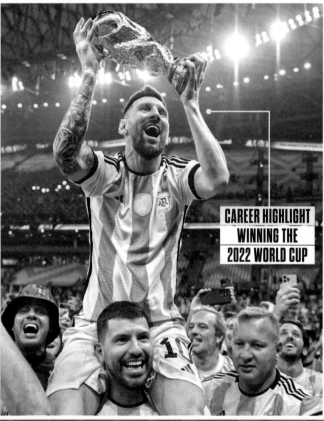
CAREER HIGHLIGHT WINNING THE 2022 WORLD CUP

*stats correct up to 1 Aug 2023

Does Messi's World Cup win in 2022 prove once and for all he's the GOAT?

BALLON D'OR AWARDS

7

GOLDEN BOOTS

6 European Golden shoes
6 Champions League top scorer
8 La Liga top scorer
1 Copa America top scorer

BEST 5 SEASONS

1	2011-12	73 goals / 60 games
2	2012-13	60 goals / 50 games
3	2014-15	58 goals / 57 games
4	2016-17	54 goals / 52 games
5	2010-11	53 goals / 55 games

40+ GOALS IN A SEASON

10 TIMES

MESSI'S TOP 3 RECORDS

Won a record 7 Ballon d'Or awards
La Liga all-time record goalscorer
Argentina all-time record goalscorer

I'M TEAM MESSI

CRISTIANO RONALDO

BORN 1985 AGE 38

BIRTHPLACE
FUNCHAL, MADEIRA, PORTUGAL

MAJOR TROPHIES

- **1** European Championship
- **1** UEFA Nations League
- **5** Champions League
- **3** Premier League
- **2** La Liga **2** Serie A
- **1** FA Cup **2** Copa del Rey
- **2** EFL Cup **1** Coppa Italia
- **4** FIFA Club World Cup
- **2** UEFA Super Cup

TOTAL TROPHIES
32

PRO DEBUT: 2002

CLUB	COUNTRY
968 GAMES	**200** GAMES
715 GOALS	**123** GOALS

TOTAL
1,168 GAMES **838** GOALS
1 GOAL EVERY 1.39 GAMES

CAREER HIGHLIGHT
WINNING A FIFTH UCL TITLE IN 2018

2002-03
5 GOALS

2003-09
118 GOALS

2009-18
450 GOALS

JUVENTUS
2018-21
101 GOALS

2021-23
27 GOALS

2023-
14 GOALS

*stats correct up to 1 Aug 2023

Does Ronaldo's better goalscoring record mean he's No.1?

BALLON D'OR AWARDS

5

GOLDEN BOOTS

4 European Golden Shoes
7 Champions League top scorer
3 La Liga top scorer
1 Premier League top scorer
1 Serie A top scorer
2 European Championship top scorer

BEST 5 SEASONS

1	2014-15		61 goals / 54 games
2	2011-12		60 goals / 55 games
3	2012-13		55 goals / 55 games
4	2010-11		53 goals / 54 games
5	2013-14		51 goals / 47 games

40+ GOALS IN A SEASON

9 TIMES

RONALDO'S TOP 3 RECORDS

■ International football all-time record goalscorer
■ Champions League all-time record goalscorer
■ Real Madrid all-time record goalscorer

I'M TEAM RONALDO

QUIZ AN ADULT!

This is your chance to see just how much your chosen adult knows about football. Are they a genuine footy brainiac, or will they crumble under the pressure? LET'S FIND OUT!

BEFORE YOU START!

YOUR ADULT WILL NEED...

- A CUP OF TEA (MAYBE EVEN A BISCUIT)
- A FULLY FUNCTIONING FOOTY MEMORY
- THEIR FAVE SLIPPERS
- A PEN

NOW IT'S YOUR TURN TO BE QUIZ MASTER!

HAND·HELD CELL PHONE USE PROHIBITED

NO CHEATING! Put that phone away!

QUIZ AN ADULT!

1 MATCH THE AWESOME FOOTY STADIUMS TO THE CORRECT BADGE!

1

2

3

4

A ....

B ....

C ....

D ....

2 NAME THESE FIVE PREMIER LEAGUE PLAYERS FROM THE 1990S!

A
....
....

B
....
....

C
....
....

D
....
....

E
....
....

3 HE'S THE LAST ENGLISH BOSS TO WIN THE LEAGUE TITLE – BUT WHAT'S HIS NAME?

....

4 WHICH CLUBS WORE THESE ICONIC SHIRTS BACK IN THE DAY?

A ....

B ....

C ....

5 WHICH PREM CLUB DID THESE FOUR GAFFERS ALL MANAGE IN THE 1990S?

....

6 WHICH CLUBS WERE THESE PREMIER LEAGUE TOP SCORERS PLAYING FOR AT THE TIME THEY WON THE GOLDEN BOOT?

A ....

B ....

C ....

D ....

E ....

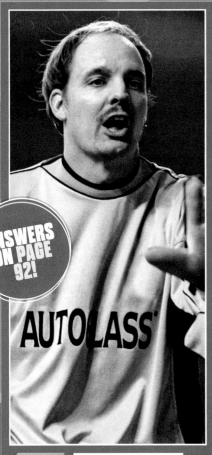

ANSWERS ON PAGE 92!

AUTOLASS

8 THIS GUY WAS NAMED IN THE PFA TEAM OF THE YEAR IN 1995-96. WHO IS HE?

....

9 NAME THIS ARGENTINIAN PLAYMAKER WHO JOINED MAN. UNITED IN 2001.

....

7 ED DE GOEY WAS IN GOAL FOR WHICH CLUB IN THE 2000 FA CUP FINAL?

....

10 THIS STRIKER WAS PFA PLAYER OF THE YEAR AND TOP SCORER IN 1987. WHAT'S HIS NAME?

....

HALF-TIME SCORE
☐ /23

QUIZ

ANSWERS ON PAGE 92!

11

THIS GUY WAS TOP SCORER AT THE 1998 WORLD CUP. WHAT'S HIS NAME?

A Milan Baros		B Davor Suker	
C Predrag Mijatovic		D Hristo Stoichkov	

14

WHAT WAS THE NAME OF THIS ICONIC WORLD CUP MASCOT?

A Goalio	
B Ciao	
C Calcio	
D Bravo	

12

WHO BEAT ARSENAL 2-1 IN THE 2006 CHAMPIONS LEAGUE FINAL?

A Real Madrid		B Barcelona		C AC Milan		D Chelsea	

13

WHICH COUNTRY DID AWESOME STRIKER SONNY ANDERSON PLAY FOR?

A South Africa	
B Sweden	
C Brazil	
D Denmark	

15

WHICH OF THESE PLAYERS DID NOT SCORE AT THE 2002 WORLD CUP?

A Sol Campbell   B Rio Ferdinand

C Emile Heskey   D Paul Scholes

16 WHO SCORED THE WINNER IN THE EURO 2008 FINAL?

A David Villa	B Andres Iniesta
C Fernando Torres	D Cesc Fabregas

17 WHICH COUNTRY WON THE 2004 EUROPEAN CHAMPIONSHIP?

A Portugal	B Denmark	C Greece	D France

18

WHO MANAGED ENGLAND AT EURO 2000?

A Glenn Hoddle	B Terry Venables	C Kevin Keegan	D Sven-Goran Eriksson

19 WHICH CLUB HAS NEVER WON THE CHAMPIONS LEAGUE?

A Porto	B Dortmund
C Marseille	D Atletico Madrid

20 WHICH 1998 WORLD CUP WINNER NEVER PLAYED IN THE PREM?

A Bixente Lizarazu	B Christian Karembeu

C Christophe Dugarry	D Youri Djorkaeff

How did you do?

FULL-TIME SCORE

/33

VINICIUS JR
BRAZIL

MATCH OF THE DAY MAGAZINE

WORLD DREAM TEAM!

FORWARD

WHO THE HECK ARE YOU?

Can you guess the *HIDDEN BALLERS* in the photos below?

Llama chop!

1
....
....

2

3

4

5

6

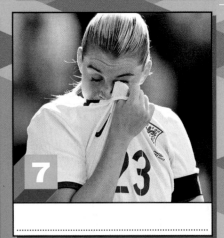

7

8

9

YOUR FOOTY BRAIN POWER

9	GENIUS
7	PROFESSIONAL
5	SEMI-PRO
3	AMATEUR
1	SUNDAY LEAGUE
0	OH NO, DISASTER

YOUR SCORE ☐ /9

ANSWERS ON PAGE 92!

KYLIAN MBAPPE

MATCH OF THE DAY MAGAZINE
WORLD DREAM TEAM!
FORWARD

THE BEST OF THE BEST!

We collect stickers, Alexia Putellas collects trophies!

We reveal the top 30 players in women's football — does YOUR hero make our list?

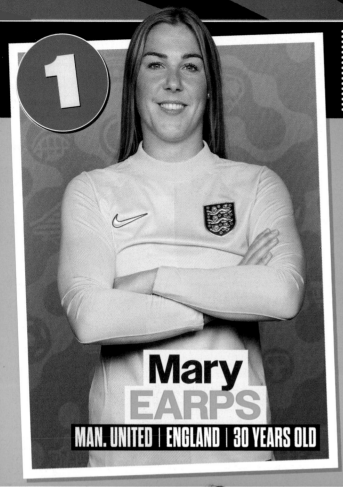

1

Mary
EARPS
MAN. UNITED | ENGLAND | 30 YEARS OLD

KEEPERS

→ Agile, commanding and brave
→ Expert decision maker with perfect passing
→ Intelligent, aware, with lightning reflexes

2

Merle
FROHMS
WOLFSBURG | GERMANY | 28 YEARS OLD

3

Christine
ENDLER
LYON | CHILE | 32 YEARS OLD

4

Sandra
PANOS
BARCELONA | SPAIN | 30 YEARS OLD

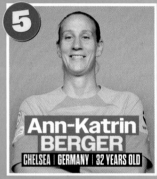

5

Ann-Katrin
BERGER
CHELSEA | GERMANY | 32 YEARS OLD

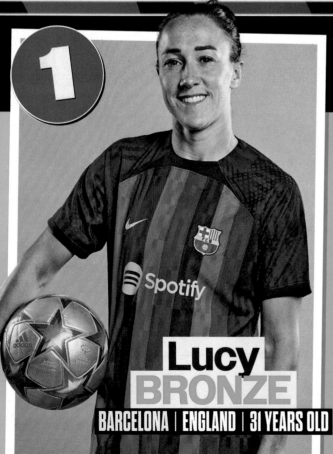

1

Lucy
BRONZE
BARCELONA | ENGLAND | 31 YEARS OLD

FULL-BACKS

→ Energetic, quick and super-fit
→ Excellent dribbling, passing and crossing skills
→ Tactically aware with positional intelligence

2

Fridolina
ROLFO
BARCELONA | SWEDEN | 29 YEARS OLD

3

Selma
BACHA
LYON | FRANCE | 22 YEARS OLD

4

Sakina
KARCHAOUI
PSG | FRANCE | 27 YEARS OLD

5

Ashley
LAWRENCE
CHELSEA | CANADA | 28 YEARS OLD

1
Irene PAREDES
BARCELONA | SPAIN | 32 YEARS OLD

CENTRE-BACKS
➔ Cool, calm and composed
➔ Big, powerful and strong
➔ Tactically and technically excellent

2 Magdalena ERIKSSON
BAYERN MUNICH | SWEDEN | 29 YEARS OLD

3 Wendie RENARD
LYON | FRANCE | 33 YEARS OLD

4 Mapi LEON
BARCELONA | SPAIN | 28 YEARS OLD

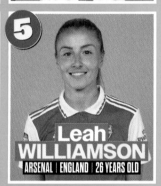

5 Leah WILLIAMSON
ARSENAL | ENGLAND | 26 YEARS OLD

1
Alexia PUTELLAS
BARCELONA | SPAIN | 29 YEARS OLD

MIDFIELDERS
➔ Great balance, vision and close control
➔ Confident, inventive and technically excellent
➔ A creative and intelligent passer

2 Aitana BONMATI
BARCELONA | SPAIN | 25 YEARS OLD

3 Lena OBERDORF
WOLFSBURG | GERMANY | 21 YEARS OLD

4 Keira WALSH
BARCELONA | ENGLAND | 26 YEARS OLD

5 Lina MAGULL
BAYERN MUNICH | GERMANY | 29 YEARS OLD

1

Beth MEAD

ARSENAL | ENGLAND | 28 YEARS OLD

FORWARDS

→ Quick feet with a locker full of tricks
→ Amazing control, technique and vision
→ Creates goals, scores goals – a game-changer

2

Caroline Graham HANSEN

BARCELONA | NORWAY | 28 YEARS OLD

3

Catarina MACARIO

CHELSEA | USA | 23 YEARS OLD

4

Pernille HARDER

BAYERN MUNICH | DENMARK | 30 YEARS OLD

5

Alexandra POPP

WOLFSBURG | GERMANY | 32 YEARS OLD

1

Sam KERR

CHELSEA | AUSTRALIA | 29 YEARS OLD

STRIKERS

→ Thunderous shot and sick technique
→ Clinical and ice-cool in front of goal
→ Outstanding movement and awareness

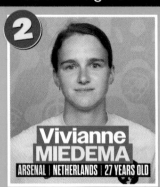

2

Vivianne MIEDEMA

ARSENAL | NETHERLANDS | 27 YEARS OLD

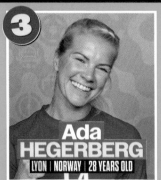

3

Ada HEGERBERG

LYON | NORWAY | 28 YEARS OLD

4

Marie-Antoinette KATOTO

PSG | FRANCE | 24 YEARS OLD

5

Asisat OSHOALA

BARCELONA | NIGERIA | 28 YEARS OLD

WHAT DO YOU THINK?

MY NO.1 KEEPER:

....

MY NO.1 FULL-BACK:

....

MY NO.1 CENTRE-BACK:

....

MY NO.1 MIDFIELDER:

....

MY NO.1 FORWARD:

....

MY NO.1 STRIKER:

....

QUIZ ANSWERS!

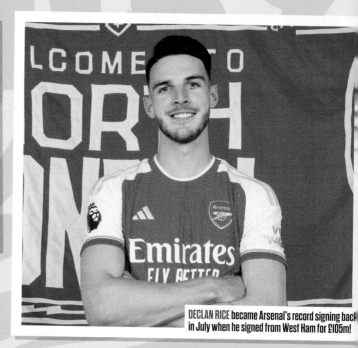

DECLAN RICE became Arsenal's record signing back in July when he signed from West Ham for £105m!

CHAMPIONS QUIZ!
From p9

1 B, 2 B, 3 C, 4 A, 5 B, 6 B, 7 B, 8 C, 9 B

MY SCORE [ ] OUT OF 9

SPOT THE BALL!
From p20

BALL ONE: 1C, BALL TWO: 1F
BALL THREE: 1B, BALL FOUR: 1G

MY SCORE [ ] OUT OF 4

STADIUM SEARCH!
From p21

MY SCORE [ ] OUT OF 12

GUESS WHO!
From p21

1 Carlo Ancelotti, 2 Pep Guardiola, 3 Erik ten Hag, 4 Mauricio Pochettino

MY SCORE [ ] OUT OF 4

BADGES & ANIMALS!
From p27

1 B, 2 C, 3 C, 4 A, 5 B, 6 C, 7 B, 8 B, 9 A

MY SCORE [ ] OUT OF 9

YEAR IN FOOTBALL!
From p39

1 C, 2 B, 3 A, 4 B, 5 B, 6 B, 7 B, 8 B, 9 C

MY SCORE [ ] OUT OF 9

BIG MONEY MEN!
From p47

1 B, 2 C, 3 B, 4 B, 5 A, 6 C, 7 A, 8 B, 9 B

MY SCORE [ ] OUT OF 9

QUIZ AN ADULT!
From p77-81

1: 1 A, 2 C, 3 B, 4 D
2: A David Batty, B Nick Barmby,
C Tim Flowers, D Dominic Matteo,
E Robbie Fowler
3 Howard Wilkinson
4: A Ipswich, B Sheffield Wednesday,
C Coventry
5 Man. City
6: A Chelsea, B Blackburn,
C Newcastle, D Man. United, E Coventry
7 Chelsea
8 Robert Lee
9 Juan Sebastian Veron
10 Clive Allen

ADULT HALF-TIME

SCORE [ ] OUT OF 23

11 B, 12 B, 13 C, 14 B, 15 D, 16 C, 17 C,
18 C, 19 D, 20 A

ADULT FULL-TIME

SCORE [ ] OUT OF 33

WHO THE HECK ARE YOU?
From p84

1 Martin Odegaard, 2 Harry Kane,
3 Mykhailo Mudryk, 4 Jarrod Bowen,
5 Erling Haaland, 6 Jordan Pickford,
7 Alessia Russo, 8 Antony,
9 Bruno Guimaraes

MY SCORE [ ] OUT OF 9

Editor Mark Parry
Deputy editor Jake Wilson
Senior art editor Blue Buxton
Senior designer Bradley Wooldridge
Annual designer Pete Rogers
Features editor Sarah Johnson

Editorial assistant Poppy Treadaway
Production editors James Bandy, Will Demetriou
Publishing Director Alex Coates-Newman
Assistant Publisher Igrain Roberts
Annual images Getty Images

Telephone 020 7150 5513
Email inbox@motdmag.com

BBC

BBC Books is an imprint of Ebury Publishing 20 Vauxhall Bridge Road London SW1V 2SA. BBC Books is part of the Penguin Random House group of companies whose addresses can be found at global.penguinrandomhouse.com. Copyright © Match Of The Day magazine 2023. First published by BBC Books in 2023 www.penguin.co.uk. A CIP catalogue record for this book is available from the British Library. ISBN 9781785948374. Commissioning editor: Albert DePetrillo, project editor: Shamanah Banerjee, production: Phil Spencer. Printed and bound in Italy by Elcograf S.p.A. The authorised representative in the EEA is Penguin Random House Ireland, Morrison Chambers, 32 Nassau Street, Dublin D02 YH68. Penguin Random House is committed to a sustainable future for our business our readers and our planet. This book is made from Forest Stewardship Council® certified paper.

MOTD Match Of The Day Magazine is published by Immediate Media Company London Limited under licence from BBC Studios Distribution Limited. © Immediate Media Company London Limited 2023.

ERLING HAALAND

NORWAY

9

MATCH OF THE DAY MAGAZINE
WORLD DREAM TEAM!
STRIKER

MY PREDICTIONS
FOR 2023-24!

We want you to make the big calls about what's going to happen this season!

MY FACT FILE!

NAME:
....

AGE: HOME TOWN:
....

FAVOURITE TEAM:
....

FAVOURITE PLAYER:
....

STICK A PHOTO OF YOURSELF HERE

1 WHO WILL WIN THE PREMIER LEAGUE?

....

Man. City have won the Prem three years in a row, and in five of the last six seasons. Can anyone stop them?

2022-23 WINNER: MAN. CITY

2 WHO WILL WIN THE GOLDEN BOOT?

....

Erling Haaland's 36 goals last term were the most scored by anyone since the Premier League began in 1992!

2022-23 WINNER: ERLING HAALAND, MAN. CITY

3 WHO WILL BE PREMIER LEAGUE PLAYER OF THE YEAR?

....

This is the award voted for by all Premier League players — it's the players' very own hero of the season!

2022-23 WINNER: ERLING HAALAND, MAN. CITY

4 WHO WILL WIN THE FA CUP?

....

The FA Cup was part two of Man. City's treble when they beat city rivals United in June 2023. A total of 44 different clubs have won the cup — but who will it be in 2024?

2022-23 WINNER: MAN. CITY

5 WHO WILL WIN THE EFL CUP?

....

This has been won by one of the Manchester clubs in seven of the last eight seasons, with City claiming five wins and United two. Who'll be celebrating this season?

2022-23 WINNER: MAN. UNITED